Unofficial GUIDES JUNIOR

Characters in Roblox

By Josh Gregory

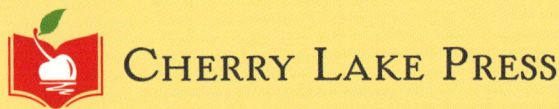

Published in the United States of America by
Cherry Lake Publishing
Ann Arbor, Michigan
www.cherrylakepublishing.com

Reading Adviser: Marla Conn MS, Ed., Literacy specialist, Read-Ability, Inc.

Copyright ©2021 by Cherry Lake Publishing
All rights reserved. No part of this book may be reproduced or
utilized in any form or by any means without written permission
from the publisher.

Library of Congress Cataloging-in-Publication Data has been filed and is available at catalog.loc.gov

Cherry Lake Publishing would like to acknowledge the work of the Partnership for 21st Century Learning,
a Network of Battelle for Kids. Please visit *http://www.battelleforkids.org/networks/p21* for more information.

Printed in the United States of America
Corporate Graphics

Table of Contents

Play It Your Way 5

Creating a Character 7

Height and Weight 9

Head to Toe 11

Colorful Characters 13

Dressing in Style 15

The Right Moves 17

Browsing the Catalog 19

Anything Goes 21

Glossary 22

Find Out More 23

Index 24

About the Author 24

What kinds of *Roblox* games do you like best? Obstacle courses like this one are very popular.

Play It Your Way

Roblox is one of the most popular video games in the world. For many players, it is more than just a game. It is a huge online sandbox. There are no limits to what you can do in *Roblox*. There are millions of different games to play. And if you don't like those, you can even make your own game. Everything in *Roblox* can be **customized** to your taste.

In this game, the player's avatar was changed to look like a character from a Japanese cartoon.

Creating a Character

Every *Roblox* player gets to create their own character. This character is called an **avatar**. You get to decide every detail of how your avatar looks. You could make a character that looks just like you. Or you could design a wild-looking avatar unlike anything you've ever seen in real life.

Different Games, Different Looks

In most *Roblox* games, you will play as your avatar. But sometimes a game will put your avatar in a funny outfit. Or you might play as a completely different character just for that game.

Avatar Editor

Explore the catalog to find more c

R6 R15

3D

Body Type   0%

Avatar isn't loading correctly?

Redraw

Recent   Clothing   Body   Animation

Body > Scale

Height

Width

Head

Proportions

You can make your avatar's body as big or small as you want.

Height and Weight

Start by choosing "Avatar" from the menu on the *Roblox* main screen. You will see all kinds of options. First, choose "Body." Then select "Scale." Here, you can change the size and **proportions** of your avatar's body. Do you want a tall, wide character? Or a short, thin one? Something in between? Play around until you have a size you like.

Avatar Editor

Body Type   0%

Avatar isn't loading correctly?
                              Redraw

Explore the catalog to find more c

Recent   Clothing   **Body**   Animations

Body > Head

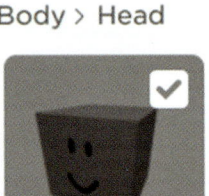

Blockhead   Woman Head   Man Head

Recommended

Roundy
By ROBLOX
Free

Chiseled
By ROBLOX
300

Cheeks
By ROBLOX
75

Trim
By ROBLOX
Free

This avatar has two different arms and a block-shaped head!

Head to Toe

You can also change the shape of your avatar's different body parts. Choose "Body." Then click on any of the body parts that are listed. You can choose different arms, legs, **torsos**, and heads. Feel free to mix and match them in any way. Want big muscular arms and kid-sized legs? A block-shaped head? Go for it!

Updated Avatars

You might notice a switch on the avatar screen that is marked "R6" on one side and "R15" on the other. R6 gives you a classic *Roblox* avatar. R15 gives you a newer style. R15 avatars have more parts. They can move in more real-looking ways than R6 avatars.

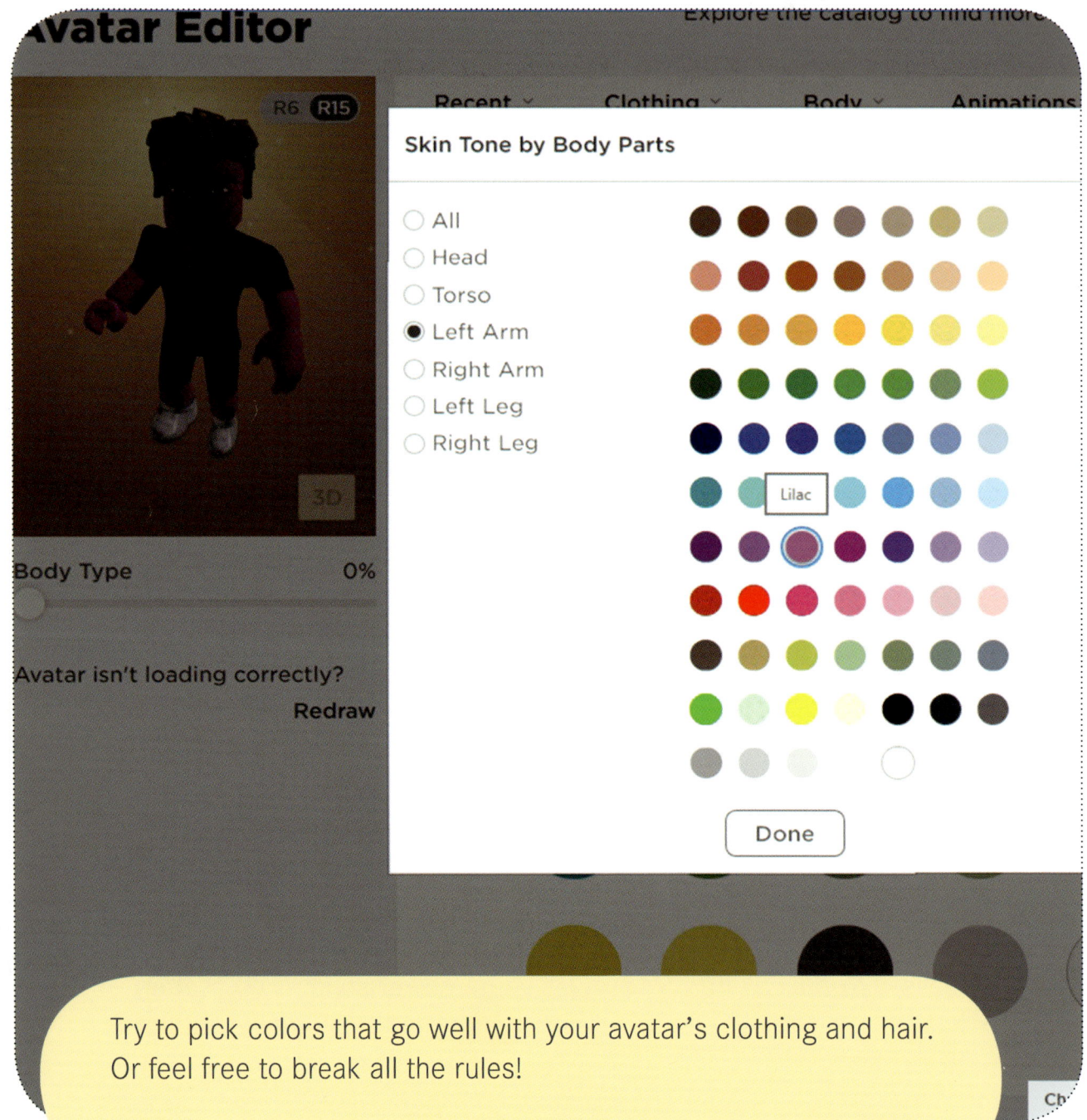

Try to pick colors that go well with your avatar's clothing and hair. Or feel free to break all the rules!

Colorful Characters

The last option in the "Body" menu is labeled "Skin Tone." Pick this to change the color of your avatar's skin. You can pick a color for your avatar's entire body. Or you can click on "Advanced." This will let you choose a different color for each body part. You could have one green arm and one purple one. Or mix orange legs with a blue head. There are no limits!

Avatar Editor

Explore the catalog to find more

Body Type   0%

Avatar isn't loading correctly?
Redraw

Recent   Clothing   Body   Animation

Clothing > Hair

Pal Hair

Straight Blonde Hair

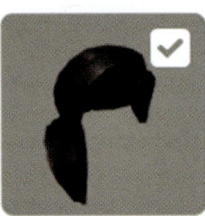
Black Ponytail

Chestnut B

Blonde Spiked Hair

Brown Charmer Hair

Recommended

Hairstyles are located in the "Clothing" section of the avatar menu. They work a lot like hats. Simply choose one and it will show up on your avatar's head.

Dressing in Style

Your avatar can wear all kinds of different clothes. The basics include pants and shirts. But you can also add different accessories. There are hats, glasses, and all kinds of jewelry. You can give your avatar a tail or wings. You can even choose a pet to ride on your avatar's shoulders. Or you can select items your avatar will carry in their hands.

Avatar Editor

Explore the catalog to find more clo

Body Type   0%

Avatar isn't loading correctly?
                        Redraw

Recent   Clothing   Body   **Animations**

Animations > Emotes

Shrug

Point2

Stadium

Hello

Recommended

Tree
By ROBLOX
◉ 80

Louder
By ROBLOX
◉ 250

Idol
By ROBLOX
◉ 500

Godlike
By ROBLOX
◉ 80

Emotes are useful for communicating with other players without using text chat.

The Right Moves

Want to change the way your avatar moves around in *Roblox* games? Choose "Animations" from the avatar screen. You can change the way your character runs, jumps, and more. For example, maybe you'd like your avatar to walk like a robot. Or run like a ninja. You can also choose which **emotes** you want to use in games. For example, you can do a dance or wave to other players.

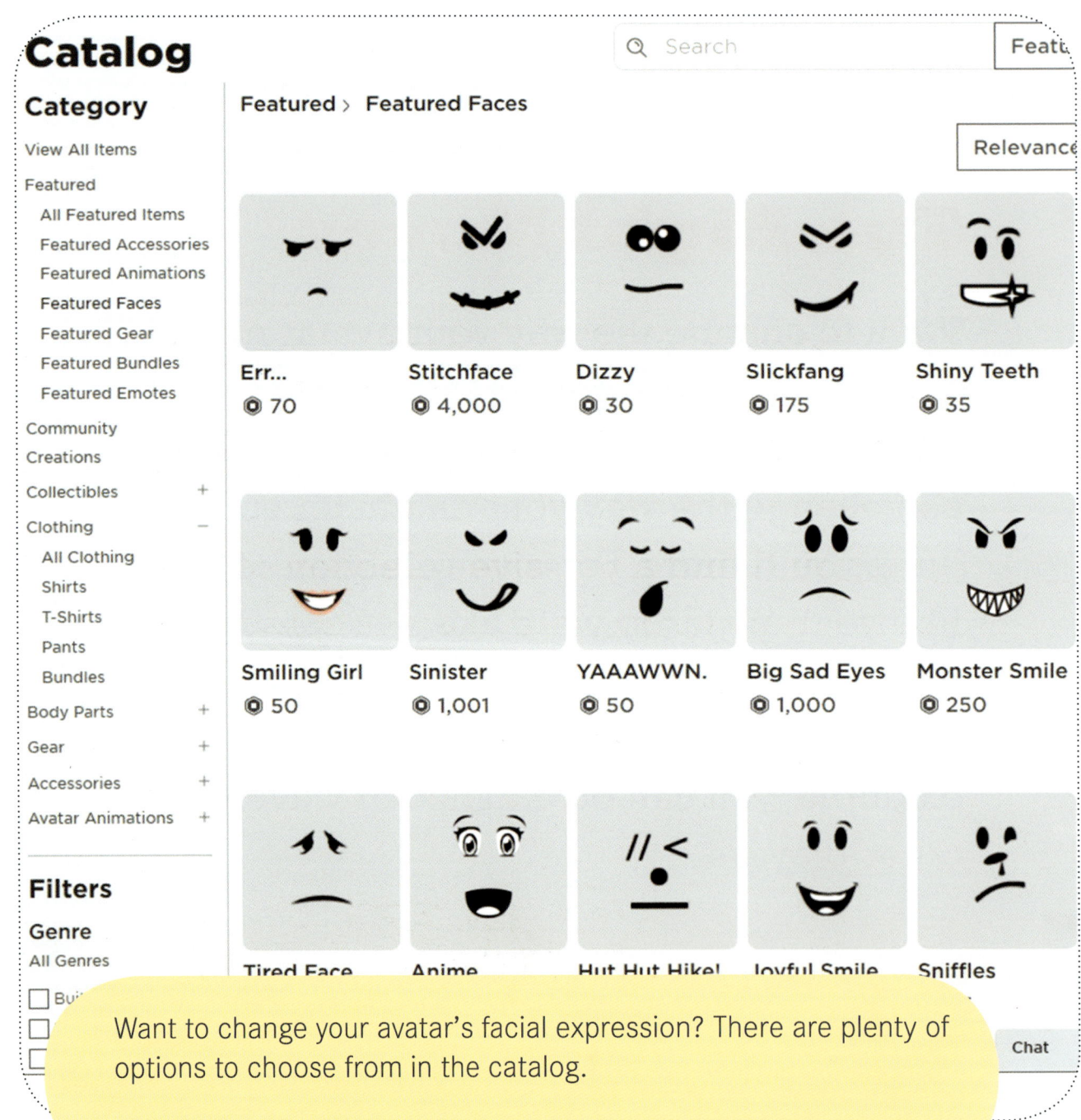

Want to change your avatar's facial expression? There are plenty of options to choose from in the catalog.

Browsing the Catalog

You will only have a few avatar style options to choose from when you start playing *Roblox*. Want to get more? Choose "Catalog" from the main *Roblox* screen. Here, you'll find a massive selection of clothes, body parts, and more. You have to purchase them using Robux. Robux are *Roblox*'s in-game money.

Spend Wisely

Remember that Robux cost real money. Just like in real life, you can't buy everything you want. Choose carefully. Only buy the things you really love!

Try using different avatar designs in different *Roblox* games.

Anything Goes

Play around with your avatar until you have a look you love. Be creative and don't be afraid to try new things. You can always change your avatar if you change your mind or get bored of it. Or maybe you'll find the perfect look for you and keep it for a long time. Like everything else in *Roblox*, it's all up to you. Have fun!

Glossary

avatar (AV-uh-tar) a character that represents you in a video game

customized (KUS-tuh-myzd) changed to meet someone's tastes or needs

emotes (EE-mohts) animated movements that a character can perform in *Roblox*

proportions (pruh-POOR-shuhns) how big something is compared to other things

torsos (TORE-sohs) the section of the body between the neck and waist, not including arms

Find Out More

Books
Cunningham, Kevin. *Video Game Designer*. Ann Arbor, MI: Cherry Lake Publishing, 2016.

Powell, Marie. *Asking Questions About Video Games*. Ann Arbor, MI: Cherry Lake Publishing, 2016.

Web Sites
Roblox
www.roblox.com
Sign up for a *Roblox* account, download the game, and start playing.

Roblox Support
https://en.help.roblox.com/hc/en-us
Find answers to common questions about *Roblox* and check out some guides to getting started.

Index

accessories, 15
"Animations" menu, 17
arms, 11, 13

"Body" menu, 9, 11, 13

"Catalog" menu, 19
clothing, 7, 15, 19
customization, 5, 7

details, 7

emotes, 17

glasses, 15

hats, 15
heads, 11, 13

jewelry, 15

legs, 11, 13

money, 19

proportion options, 9

"R6" options, 11
"R15" options, 11
Robux, 19

size options, 9, 11
skin tone, 13

tails, 15
torsos, 11

wings, 15

About the Author

Josh Gregory is the author of more than 150 books for kids. He has written about everything from animals to technology to history. A graduate of the University of Missouri–Columbia, he currently lives in Chicago, Illinois.